W9-AUX-920

Chinese Giant Salamander

The World's Biggest Amphibian

by Ann O. Squire

Consultants:

Michael Lau
Kadoorie Farm and Botanic Garden
Hong Kong, China

Meredith Whitney
Herpetology and Conservation Manager
The Maryland Zoo in Baltimore
Baltimore, MD

BEARPORT
PUBLISHING

New York, New York

Credits

Cover, ©Ken Lucas/ARDEA LONDON; 2–3, ©2003 Giant Salamander Protection International Organization; 4, Kathrin Ayer; 4–5, ©Daniel Heuclin/NHPA; 6–7, ©Zou Haibin/Imagine China; 8, ©Shanghai Daily/Imagine China; 9BKG, ©Siegfried Martin/Bilderberg/Peter Arnold; 10, ©Zou Haibin/Imagine China; 11, ©Karl Switak/NHPA; 12 (inset), ©Werner Krutein/Photovault.com; 12–13, ©2003 Giant Salamander Protection International Organization; 14 (inset), ©Werner Krutein/Photovault.com; 14–15, ©Werner Krutein/Photovault.com; 16–17, ©Zigmund Lesxczynski/Animals Animals/Earth Scenes/Oxford Scientific; 18, ©2003 Giant Salamander Protection International Organization; 19, ©Shiu Xiaojie/Imagine China; 20, ©Shai Ginot/Corbis; 21, ©Song Jianchun/Imagine China; 22L, ©Robert Irwin/NHPA; 22C, ©Daniel Heuclin/NHPA; 22R, ©Mark Bowler/NHPA; 23TL, ©Jean Michel Labat/Peter Arnold; 23TR, ©David R. Frazier/Photo Researchers; 23BL, ©Buddy Mays/Corbis; 23BR, ©Karl Switak/NHPA; 23BKG, ©Siegfried Martin/Bilderberg/Peter Arnold.

Publisher: Kenn Goin
Project Editor: Lisa Wiseman
Editorial Development: Nancy Hall, Inc.
Creative Director: Spencer Brinker
Photo Researcher: Carousel Research, Inc.: Mary Teresa Giancoli
Design: Otto Carbajal

Library of Congress Cataloging-in-Publication Data

Squire, Ann.
Chinese giant salamander : the world's biggest amphibian / by Ann O. Squire.
  p. cm.—(SuperSized!)
Includes bibliographical references and index.
ISBN-13: 978-1-59716-386-6 (library binding)
ISBN-10: 1-59716-386-4 (library binding)
1. Chinese giant salamander—Juvenile literature. I. Title.

QL668.C24S68 2007
597.8'5—dc22
                              2006032252

For more information, write to Bearport Publishing Company, Inc., 101 Fifth Avenue, Suite 6R, New York, New York 10003. Printed in the United States of America.

10 9 8 7 6 5 4 3 2

Contents

Super Salamander

The Chinese giant salamander is the biggest **amphibian** in the world.

A Chinese giant salamander is about as long as a dolphin.

A Chinese giant salamander can grow up to 8 feet (2.4 m) long. It can weigh up to 140 pounds (64 kg).

An Unusual Amphibian

All amphibians start their lives in water.

Most of them live on land when they grow up.

The giant salamander is different from many other amphibians.

It spends nearly its whole life underwater.

These giant salamanders don't take in air through their mouths. They get air through their moist skin.

At Home in China

The giant salamander lives in the mountain streams of China.

It hides in water-filled caves under the water.

During the day the salamander sleeps.

At night it hunts for food.

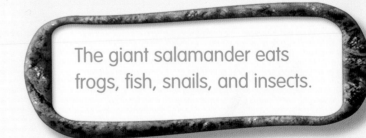

The giant salamander eats frogs, fish, snails, and insects.

Chinese Giant Salamanders in the Wild

Asia

China

Pacific Ocean

Indian Ocean

Where Chinese giant salamanders live

Fast Food

When hunting, the giant salamander hides between rocks.

It waits for **prey** to swim by.

When an animal gets close, the salamander gulps it down.

The salamander uses its mouth like a vacuum cleaner to suck in food.

Slippery Skin

The giant salamander has a wrinkly body.

Its skin is covered with a slippery coating.

This coating protects the salamander from getting hurt.

skin

A salamander's skin is brown, green, or black. In very few cases, the skin can be pink or yellow.

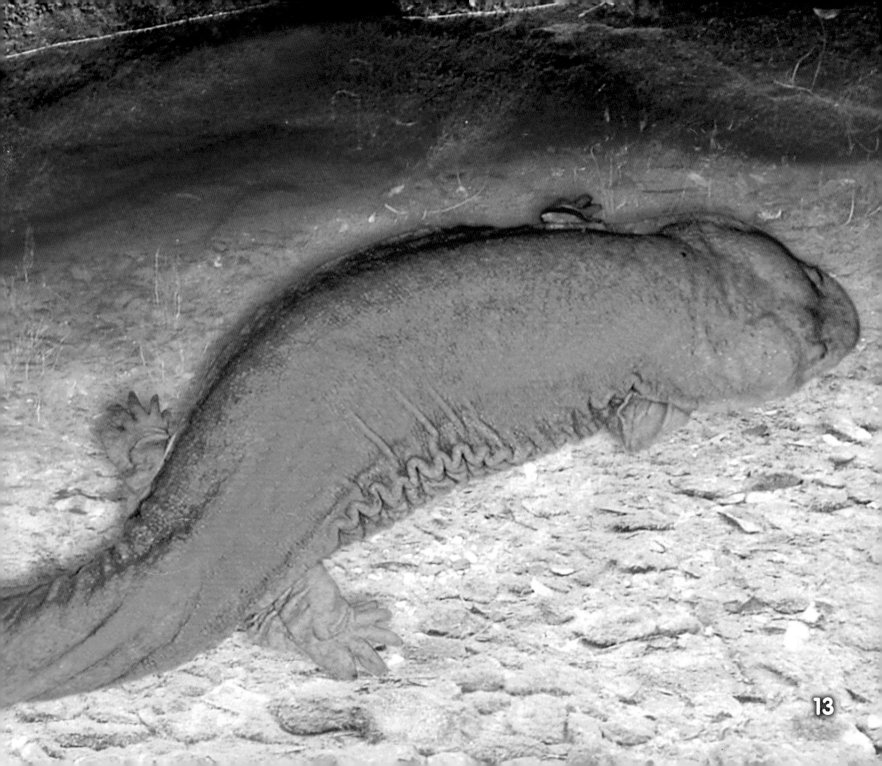

Feeling Its Way

The salamander's eyes are on top of its head.

They are so small that the salamander can hardly see.

The salamander cannot use its eyes to look for food.

It uses its sense of smell and of touch.

eye

Giant salamanders do not have eyelids.

Silent Salamanders

Giant salamanders do not make sounds.

In the past, people thought these big salamanders could cry like a baby.

Scientists now know this is not true.

Chinese giant salamanders don't make sounds because they don't have vocal cords.

Giant Parents, Tiny Babies

Female salamanders lay their eggs in underwater caves.

Males guard the eggs.

When the babies hatch, they are about 1 inch (2.5 cm) long.

The tiny babies go off to live on their own.

A female salamander lays between 350 and 500 eggs at one time.

baby
salamander

Salamanders in Danger

In China, people sometimes hunt these salamanders for food.

Water **pollution** and **dams** harm the streams where they live.

Now, scientists are studying the giant salamanders.

They are finding ways to protect these big amphibians.

Chinese giant salamanders can live to be about 55 years old.

dam

More Big Amphibians

Chinese giant salamanders belong to a group of animals called amphibians. All amphibians are cold-blooded and start their lives in water. Most amphibians move to dry land when they grow up. Others stay in or near water.

Here are three more big amphibians.

Hellbender

The hellbender is a salamander that lives in North America. It can grow to be more than 2 feet (61 cm) long.

Goliath Frog

The Goliath frog can grow to be about 1 foot (30 cm) long.

Cane Toad

The cane toad can grow to be about 9 inches (23 cm) long.

Chinese Giant Salamander: 8 feet/2.4 m

Hellbender:
2 feet/61 cm

Goliath Frog:
1 foot/30 cm

Cane Toad:
9 inches/23 cm

Glossary

amphibian
(am-FIB-ee-uhn)
an animal that is
born and lives in
water while it is
young; most live
on land when
they grow up

pollution
(puh-LOO-shuhn)
harmful waste,
such as trash, that
gets into water,
soil, and air,
making them
unsafe for living
things

dams (DAMZ)
structures built
across rivers or
streams to hold
back water

prey (PRAY)
an animal that is
hunted by other
animals for food

Index

Read More

Patkau, Karen. *Creatures Great and Small.* Toronto, Canada: Tundra Books (2006).

Taylor, Barbara. *Animal Giants.* Boston, MA: Kingfisher (2004).

Theodorou, Rod. *Amphibians.* Chicago, IL: Heinemann (1999).

Learn More Online

To learn more about Chinese giant salamanders, visit

www.bearportpublishing.com/SuperSized